CARTOONING IN COLOUR

WITH

PETER COUPE

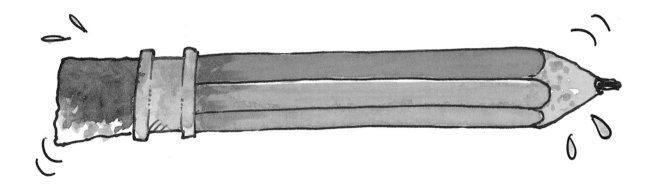

THIS EDITION PUBLISHED

by ARCTURUS PUBLISHING LTD
for BOOKMART LIMITED
REGISTERED NUMBER: 2372865
DESFORD ROAD
ENDERBY
LEICESTER
LE9 5AD

©ARCTURUS PUBLISHING/PETER COUPE/2000

ISBN. 1 84193 012 1

CONTENTS...

PENCIL AT THE
READY • • •

LET'S **GO** ➔

FUNNY FACES....

DRAWING FUNNY FACES IS **EASY** – AND LOTS OF **FUN.** FOLLOW THE SIMPLE EXAMPLES ON THE NEXT FEW PAGES, AND YOU'LL SOON BE ABLE TO DRAW **ALL** THE FUNNY FACES YOU WILL **EVER** NEED ➤

START YOUR FACE BY DRAWING THREE 'BLOBS' — LIKE THIS.

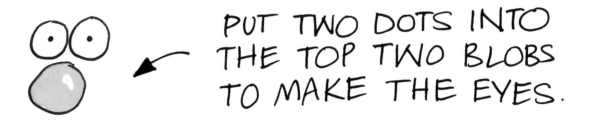

PUT TWO DOTS INTO THE TOP TWO BLOBS TO MAKE THE EYES.

NOW - DRAW A LONG CURVE UNDERNEATH — YOU'VE DRAWN A HAPPY FACE**!**

WE'LL USE THE SAME THREE BLOBS TO START **ALL** OUR FACES - NOW LET'S TRY **SOME MORE** ➤

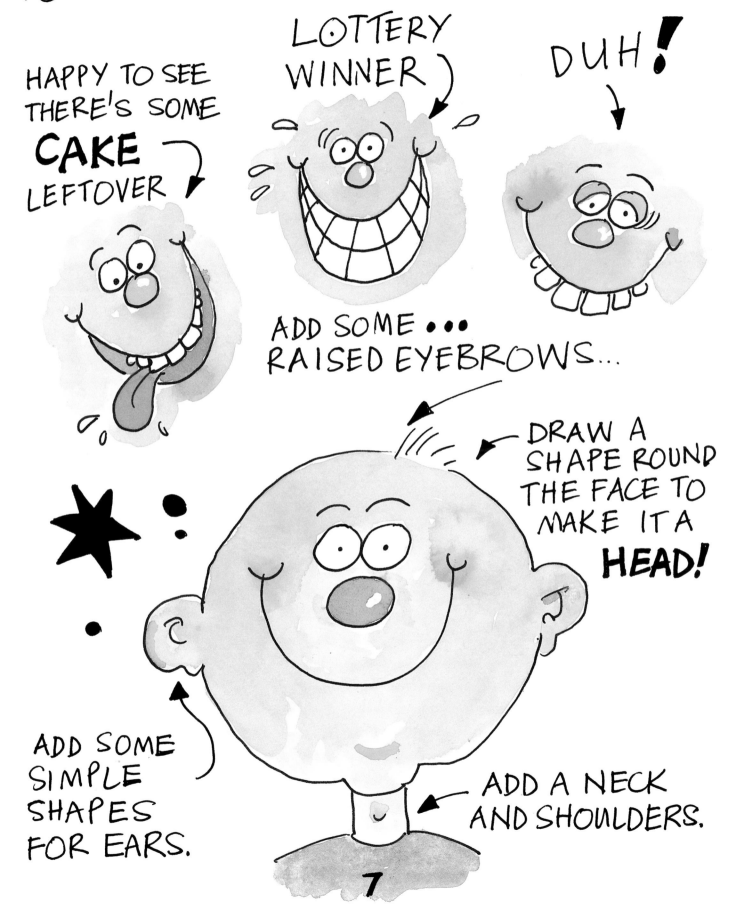

HERE ARE A FEW MORE **HAPPY** FACES FOR **YOU** TO TRY...

HAPPY TO SEE THERE'S SOME **CAKE** LEFTOVER

LOTTERY WINNER

DUH**!**

ADD SOME... RAISED EYEBROWS...

DRAW A SHAPE ROUND THE FACE TO MAKE IT A **HEAD!**

ADD SOME SIMPLE SHAPES FOR EARS.

ADD A NECK AND SHOULDERS.

7

IF YOU WANT TO DRAW FACES FROM THE SIDE, DO IT LIKE THIS...

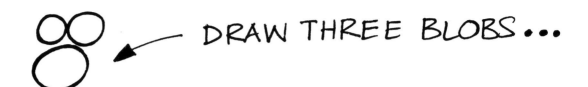 DRAW THREE BLOBS...

DRAW DOTS IN THE TOP BLOBS TO MAKE EYES...

 DRAW HALF A CURVE UNDER THE BOTTOM BLOB....

JOIN THE CURVE TO THE BOTTOM BLOB—ADD A FACE SHAPE AND ONE EAR.

SOME CARTOON ARTISTS ONLY DRAW ONE EYE IN THE SIDE VIEW— I DRAW TWO!

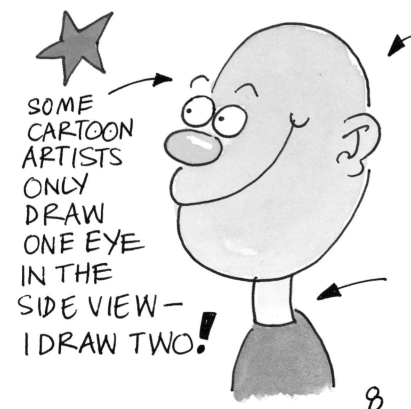

YOU CAN ADD A NECK AND SHOULDERS LIKE BEFORE.

HERE ARE SOME HAPPY FACES FROM MY CARTOONS

* HE IS LAUGHING SO HARD – HIS EYES ARE ALL SCRUNCHED UP

TRY SOME HAPPY FACES FOR YOURSELF.

9

NOW - WE'LL DRAW A **SAD** FACE...

 ← START WITH 3 BLOBS.
ADD THE DOTS IN THE TOP
BLOBS FOR THE EYES -
THEN DRAW A LINE ACROSS
THE MIDDLE OF THE EYES.

 ← A LONG CURVE - THIS
TIME POINTING DOWN
AT THE ENDS - GIVES US
A MISERABLE FACE.

 ← YOU CAN ALSO ADD
SOME SAD LOOKING
EYEBROWS TO COMPLETE
THE EFFECT!

★

ON THE NEXT PAGE ARE SOME
MORE FACES FOR YOU TO TRY
FOR YOURSELF...

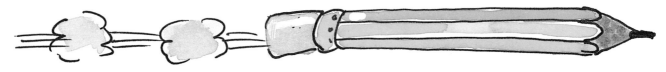

TRY SOME OF **THESE** SAD FACES...

* TEARS

* WOBBLY CHIN

GLOOM

SOMETIMES CARTOONISTS ADD A CLOUD OF GLOOM TO MAKE THE FACE EVEN **MORE MISERABLE!**

O.K! THAT'S ENOUGH SADNESS!

ANGRY FACES ARE FUN TO DRAW...

WE USE OUR THREE BLOBS, BUT DRAW THE EYEBROWS AS **DARK** DIAGONAL LINES.

DRAW THE MOUTH SHOWING LOTS OF ANGRY **TEETH!**

TO MAKE THIS "**EXTRA** ANGRY" FACE —

DRAW STEAM COMING OUT OF THE EARS, DARK PATCHES UNDER THE EYES, AND BEADS OF SWEAT FLYING OFF THE FOREHEAD!

PHEW!!

NEXT PAGE **NOW!**

SURPRISED FACES ARE **REALLY** EASY . . .

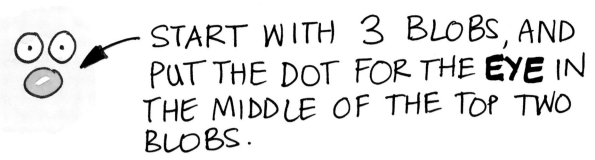 START WITH 3 BLOBS, AND PUT THE DOT FOR THE **EYE** IN THE MIDDLE OF THE TOP TWO BLOBS.

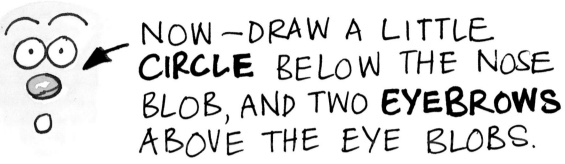 NOW—DRAW A LITTLE **CIRCLE** BELOW THE NOSE BLOB, AND TWO **EYEBROWS** ABOVE THE EYE BLOBS.

DON'T BE SO SURPRISED –
I **TOLD** YOU IT WAS **EASY!**

13

THERE ARE LOTS MORE FACES YOU CAN MAKE BY **MIXING** UP THE DIFFERENT FACES•••

CONFUSED

BORED

PLOTTING REVENGE

NOT AT ALL WELL❗

NOW– IT'S YOUR TURN➔

On THIS PAGE I HAVE DRAWN SOME "EMPTY" FACES FOR YOU TO TRY OUT YOUR NEW DRAWING SKILLS • • • •

HAVE FUN!

STICK FIGURES

THE EASIEST – AND **BEST** – WAY TO LEARN TO DRAW BRILLIANT CARTOON BODIES – START WITH **STICK** FIGURES!

IT'S EASY – **HERE'S HOW** ►►

LET'S START BY DRAWING A SIMPLE STICK FIGURE SKELETON ....

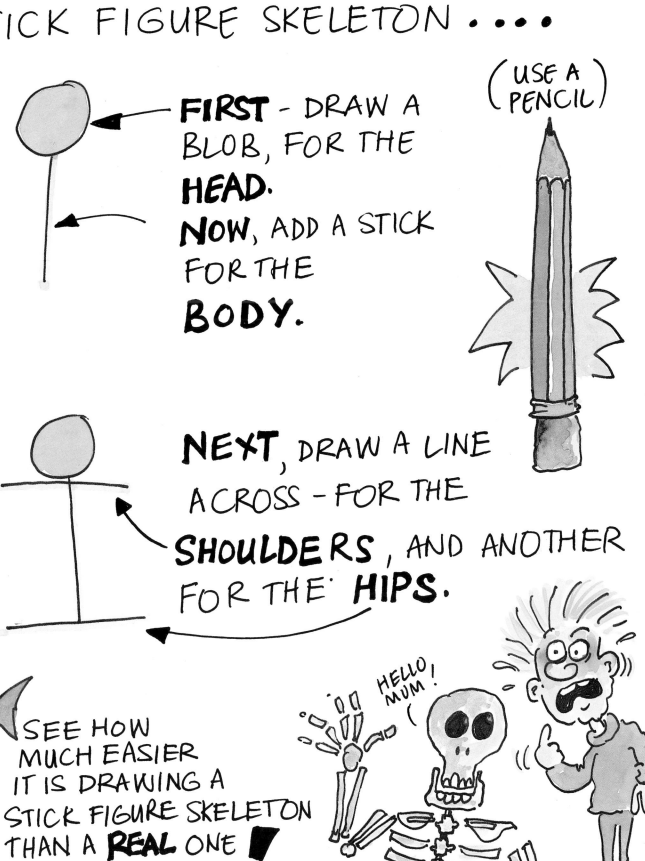

FIRST - DRAW A BLOB, FOR THE **HEAD**.
NOW, ADD A STICK FOR THE **BODY**.

(USE A PENCIL)

NEXT, DRAW A LINE ACROSS - FOR THE **SHOULDERS**, AND ANOTHER FOR THE **HIPS**.

SEE HOW MUCH EASIER IT IS DRAWING A STICK FIGURE SKELETON THAN A **REAL** ONE **!**

HELLO MUM!

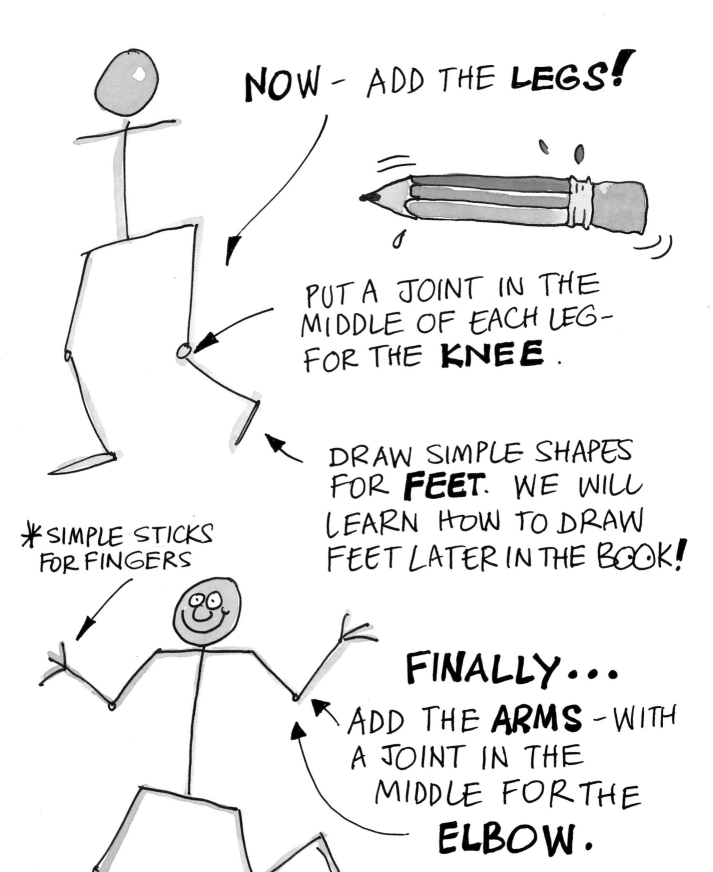

NOW - ADD THE **LEGS!**

PUT A JOINT IN THE MIDDLE OF EACH LEG- FOR THE **KNEE**.

DRAW SIMPLE SHAPES FOR **FEET**. WE WILL LEARN HOW TO DRAW FEET LATER IN THE BOOK!

✱ SIMPLE STICKS FOR FINGERS

FINALLY...

ADD THE **ARMS** - WITH A JOINT IN THE MIDDLE FOR THE **ELBOW**.

LET'S GIVE OUR SIMPLE STICK FIGURES SOME THINGS TO DO ➡

18

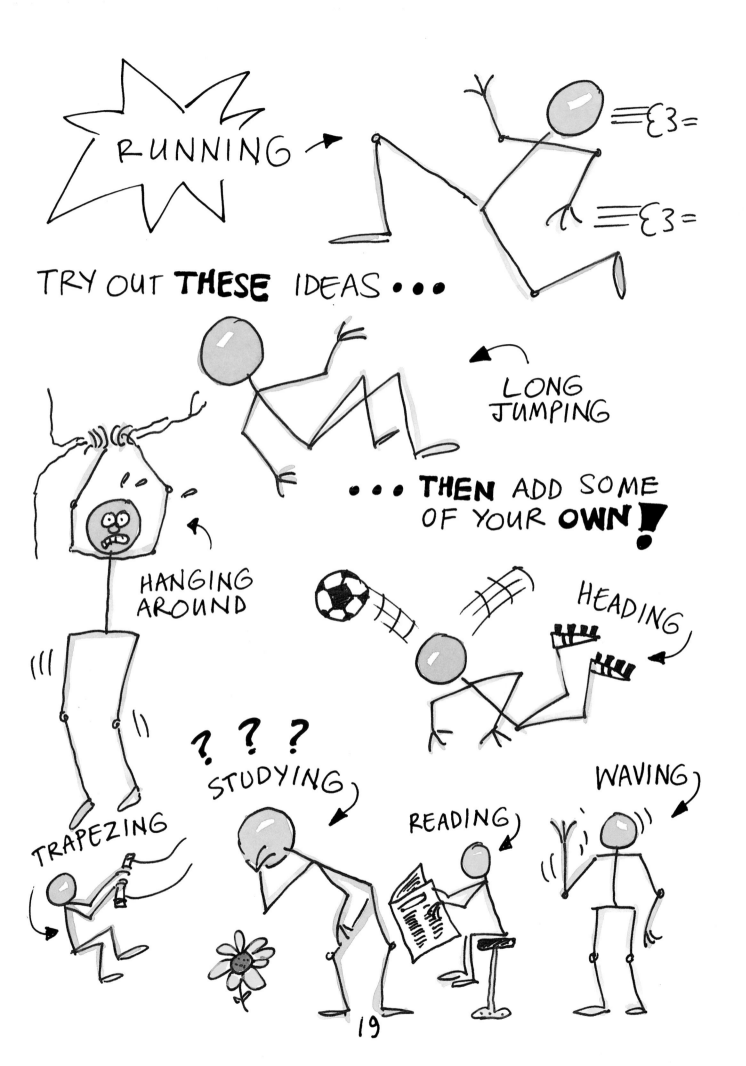

RUNNING

TRY OUT **THESE** IDEAS...

LONG JUMPING

...**THEN** ADD SOME OF YOUR **OWN!**

HANGING AROUND

HEADING

TRAPEZING

? ? ?
STUDYING

READING

WAVING

YOU CAN **TRACE** SHAPES FOR YOUR STICK FIGURES FROM NEWSPAPERS OR MAGAZINES...

PUT A SHEET OF **THIN** PAPER OVER THE PICTURE AND TRACE THE SHAPES**!**

OR...

YOU COULD **MAKE** YOUR OWN STICK FIGURE WITH TWIGS OR PENCILS OR LOLLY STICKS OR CARD ➔

IF YOU ARE REALLY **CLEVER** YOU CAN JOIN ALL THE PARTS WITH PAPER FASTENERS.

(**TAPE** OVER ANY SHARP EDGES WHEN YOU'VE DONE.)

ONCE YOU ARE HAPPY WITH THE STICK FIGURE YOU CAN DRAW SOME **CLOTHES** ON IT

JUST USE **SIMPLE** SHAPES TO BEGIN WITH, AND ADD DETAILS WHEN YOU FEEL **MORE** CONFIDENT**!**

WHEN YOU ARE HAPPY WITH THE FINAL SHAPE YOU CAN **RUB OUT** THE PENCIL STICK FIGURE—AND NO-ONE WILL KNOW **HOW** YOU DID IT**!**

WOW**!**

PROUD

HERE ARE SOME FINISHED EXAMPLES...

TRY SOME FOR YOURSELF ...

ONCE YOU'VE GOT THE HANG OF DRAWING THESE **SIMPLE** STICK FIGURES — WHY NOT TRY RINGING A FEW CHANGES ?•••••

EXTRA WIDE SHOULDERS FOR SUPER **HEROES**!

WOW! IT'S SUPER MUM!

YOU CAN CHANGE ANY PART OF YOUR CARTOONS TO SUIT YOURSELF...

BRILLIANT!

23

WHY NOT **TRY**...

SUPER LONG ARMS OR LEGS...

BIG HEADS ON TINY BODIES...

IT'S YOUR CARTOON - SO YOU CAN DO ANYTHING!

NOW - IT'S YOUR TURN

24

HERE ARE SOME STICK FIGURES FOR **YOU** TO COMPLETE • ● • •

NOW- WE CAN DRAW FANTASTIC **FACES** AND BRILLIANT **BODIES** - SO LET'S **COMPLETE** OUR CARTOON FIGURES WITH **HANDS** AND **FEET!**

 **HOW** CAN A BUNCH OF **BANANAS** HELP **YOU** TO DRAW CARTOONS**?**

 TURN THE PAGE AND FIND OUT ➡

THE EASIEST WAY I KNOW TO DRAW **HANDS** IS TO START • • • •

...BY DRAWING A SIMPLE **BUNCH** OF BANANAS **!**

NEXT – MAKE THE **STALK** INTO A **WRIST**, SMOOTH OUT THE **FINGERS** AND ADD A **THUMB!**

FLIP THE HAND OVER AND DRAW IT THE OTHER WAY UP

FINALLY –ADD WHATEVER **DETAILS** YOU FANCY •• • •

FINGERNAILS WRINKLES RINGS • • • •

REMEMBER TO KEEP IT SIMPLE **!**

I USUALLY DRAW MY CARTOON HANDS WITH **THREE** FINGERS AND A THUMB — IT JUST LOOKS BETTER TO **ME** LIKE THAT ⟶

1
2
3

EXPERIMENT WITH DIFFERENT **HAND** SHAPES UNTIL YOU FIND ONE **YOU LIKE**!

BUT...

...TRY NOT TO GET **TOO** CARRIED AWAY!

PRACTISE...
DRAWING LOTS OF HANDS — YOU WILL USE **PLENTY** OF THEM IN YOUR CARTOONS!

DRAWING **FEET** IS EASY, TOO!

START OUT WITH SOME **SIMPLE** SHAPES,
LIKE THESE ● ● ● ●

YOU CAN USE **WHATEVER** SHAPE YOU **LIKE** -
BUT REMEMBER TO PUT A HEEL ON THE
FOOT - IT **LOOKS** MUCH BETTER!

PRACTISE
DRAWING
LOTS OF DIFFERENT
SHOES ● ● ● ● ● ...

REMEMBER
THAT FEET
COME IN PAIRS ...

WHEN YOU DRAW BARE **FEET** - LIKE THIS

REMEMBER THAT THE **BIG TOE** POINTS **UP** ↑

THE OTHER TOES POINT **DOWN** ↓

PHEW!

SHOES AND FEET CAN BE **FUNNY** IN A CARTOON - HERE ARE SOME MORE FOR **YOUR** COLLECTION

ONCE YOU HAVE MASTERED THE **BASICS** OF CARTOON DRAWING, YOU WILL WANT TO **CREATE** CARTOON CHARACTERS OF YOUR **OWN**.

SO - LET'S LEARN HOW TO **DRESS** UP OUR CARTOON CREATIONS • •••• ••

GGrrr

OOPS!

NO - NOT LIKE THIS!

NEXT PAGE, QUICK!

KEEP AN **EYE** ON FASHION - **LOOK** AT WHAT PEOPLE ARE WEARING... HAIRSTYLES ....

MUSIC...

MAKE-UP...
EARRINGS...

HATS...

BEARDS...

AND REMEMBER — YOU CAN ...
EXAGGERATE ANYTHING **YOU** WANT

IF YOU WANT TO DRAW LOTS OF **DIFFERENT** PEOPLE IN YOUR CARTOONS — DRAW PEOPLE IN . . .

UNIFORM

CARTOON CHARACTERS ARE MUCH MORE **FUN** WHEN THEY ARE DOING SOMETHING ○ ○ ○ ○

LIKE **THIS LOT** ● ● ● ●...

SUCH AS ○○○

→

READING
WALKING
RUNNING
JUMPING
'PHONING
BOXING
SAILING
JUDO
SHOPPING
EATING
DRINKING
SWIMMING
LAUGHING
CRYING

ETC ETC ETC

SSSSSSS   SSSSSSSSS

SSSSSSS

SSSSSSS

MAKE YOUR CARTOON CHARACTERS AS **ACTIVE** AS POSSIBLE **!**

ADDING **COLOUR** TO YOUR CARTOONS.

COLOUR WILL BRING YOUR CARTOONS TO LIFE —AND MAKE THEM LOOK PROFESSIONAL!

THERE ARE **THREE** PRIMARY COLOURS:-

THEY ARE •••

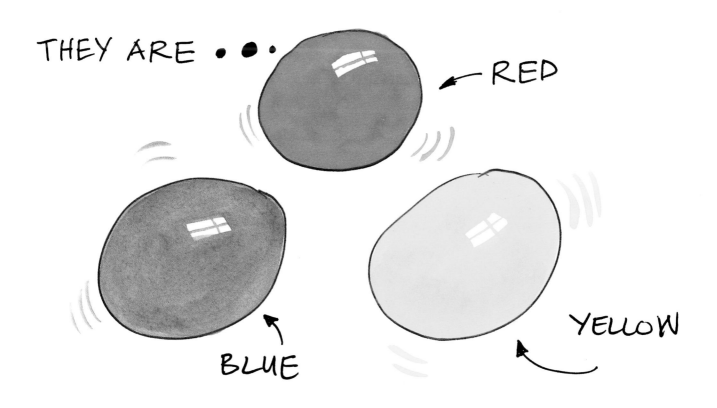

← RED

BLUE

YELLOW

DEFINITION ···

A PRIMARY COLOUR IS ONE THAT CAN'T BE MADE BY MIXING ANY OTHER COLOURS!

IF WE THEN **MIX** THE THREE PRIMARY COLOURS, WE GET **ANOTHER** THREE COLOURS...

RED AND YELLOW MAKES **ORANGE**

RED AND BLUE MAKES **PURPLE**.

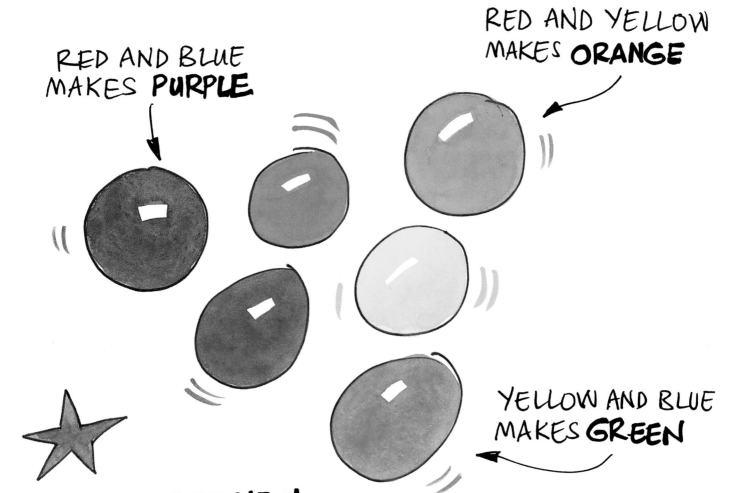

YELLOW AND BLUE MAKES **GREEN**

THESE THREE **NEW** COLOURS ARE CALLED **SECONDARY** COLOURS.

YOU CAN CARRY ON MIXING COLOURS LIKE THIS TO MAKE **LOTS** OF OTHERS....

TRY IT YOURSELF**!**

THERE ARE **LOTS** OF DIFFERENT WAYS TO
ADD COLOUR TO **YOUR** FINISHED CARTOONS.

FELT-TIPPED PENS

THESE ARE INEXPENSIVE
AND QUICK — BUT IT IS
QUITE DIFFICULT TO MIX
COLOURS WITH THEM.

THIS IS A BLOCK OF **RED**
COLOUR APPLIED WITH A
FELT TIPPED PEN.

THIS IS A BLOCK OF **BLUE**.

TO MAKE **PURPLE** —
DRAW A SERIES OF RED LINES,
THEN DRAW A SERIES OF
BLUE LINES BETWEEN THEM.

YOU CAN USE THE SAME TECHNIQUE WITH
COLOURED **PENCILS**

A LOT OF CARTOONISTS USE **WATER COLOURS...**

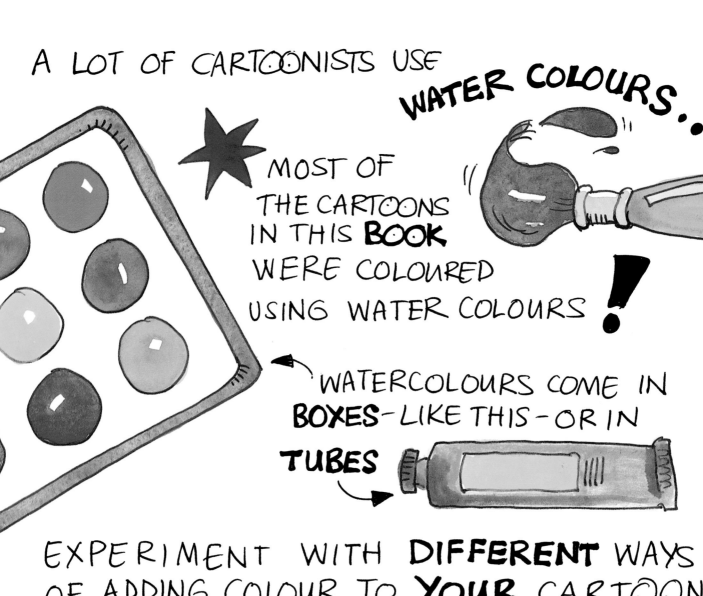

MOST OF THE CARTOONS IN THIS **BOOK** WERE COLOURED USING WATER COLOURS **!**

WATERCOLOURS COME IN **BOXES** - LIKE THIS - OR IN **TUBES**

EXPERIMENT WITH **DIFFERENT** WAYS OF ADDING COLOUR TO **YOUR** CARTOONS.

IN **THIS** CARTOON I HAVE USED WATER COLOUR, FELT PENS **AND** COLOURED PENCILS **!**

TIME TO GIVE OUR COLOURFUL CARTOON CREATIONS SOMEWHERE TO **LIVE** ° ° ° °
YOU ONLY NEED TO DRAW A **FEW** THINGS IN YOUR CARTOON TO SHOW PEOPLE WHERE THE CARTOON IS SET • • • •

IF YOU HAD **THESE** THINGS IN YOUR CARTOON IT WOULD BE EASY TO WORK OUT THAT IT WAS SET IN THE **LOUNGE** OF A HOUSE **!**

NOW - DRAW SOME THINGS FROM DIFFERENT ROOMS IN **YOUR** HOUSE.
KITCHEN • BATHROOM • BEDROOM • ETC...

HERE ARE SOME IDEAS OF **MINE** — CAN YOU WORK OUT WHERE **THESE** THINGS BELONG?

ANSWERS 1 = SCHOOLROOM   2 = KITCHEN   3 = DESERT ISLAND

IF YOU FIND IT DIFFICULT TO DRAW SOMETHING, TRY REDUCING IT TO **SIMPLE** SHAPES FIRST •••

A TRIANGLE, A SQUARE AND A RECTANGLE GIVE ME THE SHAPES I NEED TO DRAW A READING **LAMP**

THIS SIMPLE **CAR** COMES FROM A FEW SIMPLE SHAPES

ONCE YOU GET INTO THE HABIT OF DRAWING REGULARLY, YOU WILL FIND IT GETS MUCH **EASIER**!

BY NOW I'M **SURE** THAT YOUR CARTOONS ARE
STARTING TO LOOK REALLY GOOD!
OVER THE NEXT FEW PAGES WE WILL LEARN
HOW TO MAKE THEM LOOK **EVEN** BETTER!

LET'S LEARN TO :-

DRAW LIKE A ••••

PROFESSIONAL!

- LAYOUT

- SHADING AND TEXTURE

- VIEWPOINT

- ADDING WORDS

- ACTION

 LET'S DO IT!

MAKE YOUR FINISHED CARTOONS LOOK
SUPER NEAT BY LAYING THEM OUT
CAREFULLY ● ● ●
USE A CLEAN SHEET OF A4 OR LETTER
SIZE PAPER FOR **EACH** DRAWING

● LEAVE A WIDE MARGIN
ROUND THE **EDGE**
OF THE PAPER

PETER COUPE

● DRAW
YOUR
CARTOON
NEATLY –
RUB OUT
ANY PENCIL
LINES.

● PUT YOUR **NAME**
IN THE CORNER

WELL DONE **!**

NOW YOUR CARTOONS
ARE LOOKING
REALLY SMART **!**

AS WELL AS USING **COLOUR** IN YOUR CARTOONS
YOU MIGHT LIKE TO TRY ADDING SOME
SHADING AND TEXTURE • • • •

TRY SOME OF THESE PATTERNS • • •

YOU CAN
USE THESE
PATTERNS
← IN COLOUR
AS WELL**!**

USE THE
LAST BOX
TO **INVENT**
YOUR OWN
PATTERN

MAKE YOUR CARTOONS REALLY SPECTACULAR
BY USING SOME EYE- CATCHING **NEW**

 VIEWPOINTS!

TO DRAW A 'BIRD'S EYE VIEW •••

DRAW A 'V' SHAPE
IN **PENCIL**. DRAW
YOUR CARTOON
INSIDE IT. RUB OUT
THE 'V' SHAPE
WHEN YOU'VE
FINISHED!

THIS IS THE
EFFECT YOU GET...
DRAMATIC STUFF!

WOW—THERE'S **MORE**

TURN THE 'V' SHAPE THE OTHER WAY UP-
AND GET A "WORM'S EYE VIEW"!

TRY SOME YOURSELF!

HERE'S THE UPSIDE DOWN 'V' SHAPE-DRAWN IN PENCIL, SO YOU CAN RUB IT **OUT** WHEN YOUR DRAWING IS **FINISHED**!

SOMETIMES, YOU WILL WANT TO ADD **WORDS** TO YOUR CARTOONS ● ● ● ●

HERE ARE SOME **TIPS** ⇲

CAPITAL LETTERS – WRITTEN NEATLY, ARE QUITE **EASY** TO READ

PUT THE WORDS INTO BUBBLES, LIKE **THIS** ❗

A "**THINKING**" BUBBLE LOOKS LIKE THIS.

AN **ANGRY** BUBBLE LOOKS LIKE THIS❗

YOU CAN ALSO USE "SPECIAL EFFECT"
WORDS LIKE **THESE** • • • •

CRACK

Z

Z

START
YOUR OWN
COLLECTION

Z

Z

BOING

ZAP

MAKE UP
SOME OF
YOUR **OWN!**

POW

M

M

★ **NOW,** LET'S SEE HOW TO ADD
ACTIONS TO OUR CARTOONS →

IF OUR CARTOON CHARACTERS WERE STANDING STILL ALL THE **TIME**, OUR CARTOONS WOULD BE VERY BORING **!**

SO - LET'S ADD SOME **ACTION**

DULL... **!**

CARTOON CHARACTERS LOOK MORE **DYNAMIC** WHEN THEY ARE LEANING FORWARDS **!**

"**ZOOM**" CLOUDS ADD EVEN MORE "SPEED" **!**

ECHO LINES SHOW THE CHARACTER IS MOVING))

WHY NOT TRY THINKING UP SOME NEW IDEAS FOR ACTION SYMBOLS **!**

AS WELL AS DRAWING PEOPLE IN YOUR CARTOONS YOU CAN ALSO HAVE FUN DRAWING •••

ANIMALS →

MONSTERS →

BIRDS →

ALIENS →

AND JUST ABOUT **ANYTHING** ELSE THAT YOU FANCY TURNING INTO A CARTOON!

FOLLOW THE **SIMPLE** DIRECTIONS ON THE NEXT FEW PAGES — AND WHO KNOWS WHAT YOU WILL BE DRAWING **NEXT** ?!

LET'S **DO IT** →

YOU CAN DRAW LOTS OF **ANIMALS** STARTING WITH THE SIMPLE FACE WE LEARNED TO DRAW AT THE START OF THIS BOOK...

3 BLOBS-REMEMBER

★ ADD TO THESE A SIMPLE ANIMAL MOUTH

YOU CAN ALSO FILL IN THE **NOSE** BLOB IN BLACK INK OR COLOUR

TO DRAW A **DOG** - ADD A PEAR-SHAPED HEAD, BIG EARS, A TONGUE AND WHISKERS

A **CAT** STARTS WITH THE SAME FACE - ADD SHARP EARS AND A ROUNDED, FLUFFY **FACE**

DRAW YOUR FAVOURITE **HAMSTER** — WITH BIG BULGING CHEEKS AND TINY ROUNDED **EARS**

AND BIG **TEETH**

STILL THE SAME SIMPLE FACE

LET YOUR IMAGINATION RUN **WILD** — AND SEE WHAT YOU COME UP WITH ● ● ● ●

A **LION** WITH A BIG SHAGGY MANE.

HE DOESN'T SCARE **ME**!!

GULP!!

A LONGER VERSION OF THE SIMPLE FACE GIVES US THIS **CHIMP**!

52

TIME NOW FOR SOME **MONSTER** CARTOON IDEAS — HUR, HUR •••

★ FRANKENSTEIN'S MONSTER STARTS WITH THE SIMPLE 'BLOB' FACE — MAKE ONE **EYE** BIGGER THAN THE OTHER — DRAW ODD EARS AS WELL, AND MAKE THE TOP OF HIS HEAD **FLAT**!

← ADD A BOLT AND LOTS OF SCARS!

WOLFMAN IS JUST A HAIRY BASIC FACE WITH FANGS — **YUCK**!

GIVE COUNT DRACULA SOME **FANGS** TOO!

(LET'S GET ONTO THE NEXT PAGE — **QUICK!**)

53

HERE ARE SOME HANDY **HINTS** TO HELP YOU
ADD SOME BATTY **BIRDS** TO YOUR CARTOONS**!**

OWLS ARE NICE AND
EASY BIRDS TO START

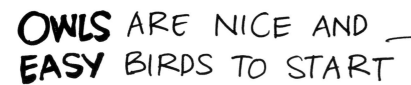

★ TWO BLOBS FOR EYES,
A TRIANGLE FOR A
BEAK. ROUNDED HEAD
AND BODY- WITH SMALL
WINGS AND LONG LEGS

DUCKS ARE **EASY** AND **FUN**, TOO — DRAW A
LONG BEAK AND A **BLOB** SHAPED HEAD;
A **FAT**, FEATHERY BODY COMPLETES
THE PICTURE ● ● ●

WHY NOT DRAW A LAKE FULL**?!**

BECAUSE NO-ONE HAS EVER SEEN ANY SPACE **ALIENS**, YOU CAN DRAW THEM ANY WAY YOU WANT TO • • • • GREAT **!**

ALIENS CAN HAVE AS MANY **EYES** AS YOU FANCY —

STRANGE, BLOBBY FINGERS —

ANTENNAE INSTEAD OF EARS —

AND **HOVER** INSTEAD OF WALKING **!**

THIS **ALSO** SAVES YOU HAVING TO DRAW FEET **!**

ONE OF THE GREAT THINGS ABOUT DRAWING CARTOONS, IS THAT YOU CAN **CREATE** YOUR VERY OWN **COMICS** AND **COMIC STRIPS**!

★ YOU CAN **USE** ANY OR ALL THE THINGS WE HAVE LEARNED TO **DRAW** SO FAR IN YOUR COMIC STRIPS AND COMICS ••••
ANIMALS ARE GOOD **FUN** - BUT THEN AGAIN SO ARE ALIENS, MONSTERS, BIRDS, **EVEN** HUMANS ! CHOICES CHOICES...

REMEMBER TO USE **LOTS** OF EXPRESSIONS.

MORE - **MORE** - MORE →

WHY NOT GO THE WHOLE HOG AND INVENT YOUR VERY OWN **COMIC** ....

FOR SPECIAL **EFFECTS** IN YOUR COMICS AND COMIC STRIPS, TRY SOME OF **THESE** •••

WHEN SOMEONE HAS A BRILLIANT **IDEA** - GIVE THEM A LIGHTBULB ABOVE THEIR HEAD TO **SHOW** IT !

SAD PEOPLE SOMETIMES HAVE A DARK CLOUD ABOVE THEM !

WAVY LINES **AND** A TWITCHY NOSE USUALLY MEAN SOMETHING **SMELLY** •••

PHEW !

COW PAT FARM

TIME NOW FOR **YOU** TO PUT ALL THE
THINGS YOU'VE LEARNED INTO **ACTION**...

THINGS TO MAKE AND DO...

CARDS...

POP-UPS...

INVITATIONS...

FACE FOLDER...

CARICATURE...

CARDS CAN BE LIKE COMIC STRIPS IN MINIATURE —

FOLD A SHEET OF A4/LETTER PAPER INTO **THREE** ...

THEN ...

DRAW A 3 PANEL CARTOON ON IT **!**

OF COURSE THE MESSAGE ON **YOUR** CARD WILL BE MUCH NICER-WON'T IT **?**

IF YOU **REALLY** WANT TO IMPRESS AS A CARD MAKER — WHY NOT **TRY** THIS **POP-UP** CARD**!**

DRAW A **SCARY** FACE — CUT IT OUT — THEN FOLD IT DOWN THE CENTRE LINE SO THE PICTURE IS INSIDE THE FOLD

FOLDED FACE

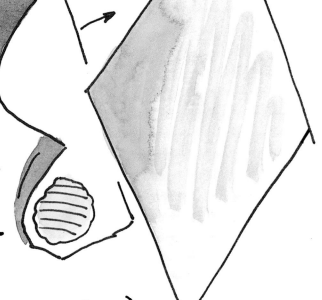

NEXT — FOLD A CLEAN SHEET OF A4/LETTER SIZED PAPER IN **HALF**

PUT A LITTLE **GLUE** ON THE FOLDED FACE

(IN THE SHADED AREA **ONLY**) AND PUT THE TWO PIECES TOGETHER . . .

WHEN THE CARD OPENS — GUESS WHO EMERGES**!?**

CARICATURE IS ANOTHER FUN WAY TO ADD INTEREST TO YOUR CARTOONS!

START WITH A FAIRLY "NORMAL" CARTOON OF YOUR INTENDED VICTIM - IN THIS CASE - ME!

THEN •••

JUST ENLARGE OR REDUCE ANY OR ALL THE FEATURES AND SEE **WHAT** YOU GET →

IN **THIS** EXAMPLE I HAVE STRETCHED THE FACE.

IN **THIS ONE** I HAVE SQUASHED IT UP

ONCE YOU HAVE SCARED YOURSELF **SILLY** DRAWING YOUR **OWN** CARICATURE – TRY DOING SOME OF YOUR FAMILY AND FRIENDS. THERE ARE ALSO **PLENTY** OF POP STARS AND CELEBRITIES TO TRY...!

JUST PICK YOUR **FAVOURITE** PERSON AND ....

...GO FOR IT!

ONCE YOU HAVE PRODUCED A CARICATURE YOU LIKE – YOU CAN **TRANSFER** IT TO A NUMBER OF OTHER THINGS ...

HERE IS **MY** CARICATURE "SELF PORTRAIT"...

AS A BRUSH

A PENCIL

A LIGHTBULB

PICK SOMETHING THAT YOU KNOW THE "SUBJECT" IS INTERESTED IN TO MAKE THE CARICATURE **PERSONAL**!

AN APPLE

65

HERE ARE A FEW THINGS YOU CAN **MAKE** USING YOUR SUPER NEW CARTOONING SKILLS ... **TRY** THIS ...

FUNNY **FACE** FOLDER

★ **FOLD** A SHEET OF A4/LETTER SIZED PAPER INTO 3 EQUAL SIZED FLAPS.

DRAW A FUNNY FACE ON THE **MIDDLE** FLAP, AND GET YOUR FRIENDS TO DRAW **FACES** ON THE OTHER TWO **!** **NEXT**...

CUT THE FLAPS INTO 3 EQUAL SIZED STRIPS — AND **FOLD !**

SEE HOW MANY **CRAZY** FACES **YOU** CAN MAKE.

CARTOON FOLDER – IS A GREAT GAME
(AND ANY NUMBER OF PEOPLE CAN **PLAY**)

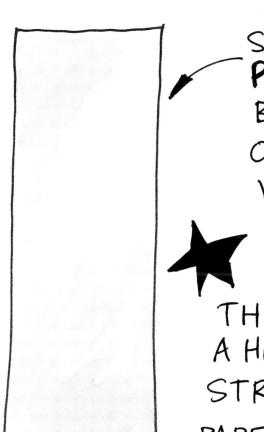

START WITH A STRIP OF **PAPER** – ANY SIZE WILL DO, BUT **HALF** A SHEET OF A4 OR LETTER SIZED PAPER WILL BE IDEAL.

THEN . . .

THE FIRST PLAYER DRAWS A HEAD AT THE TOP OF THE STRIP – THEN **FOLDS** THE PAPER, SO THE HEAD IS **HIDDEN**.

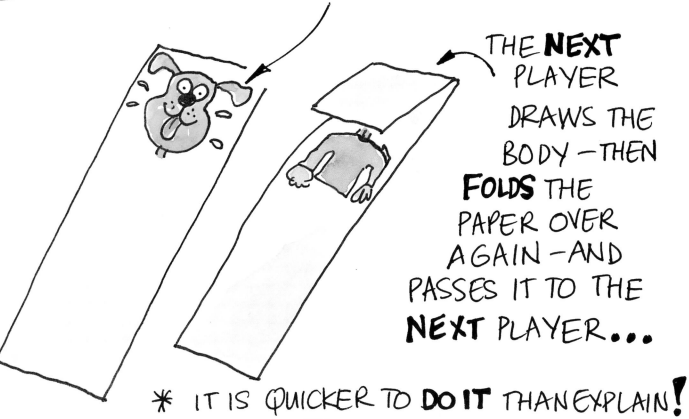

THE **NEXT** PLAYER DRAWS THE BODY – THEN **FOLDS** THE PAPER OVER AGAIN – AND PASSES IT TO THE **NEXT** PLAYER . . .

* IT IS QUICKER TO **DO IT** THAN EXPLAIN!

KEEP PASSING THE PAPER FROM PLAYER TO PLAYER UNTIL THE **FIGURE** IS COMPLETE!

NOW...

OPEN OUT THE COMPLETED DRAWING, AND SEE WHAT YOU HAVE **CREATED**!

THE **MORE** PEOPLE YOU HAVE PLAYING - THIS CRAZY GAME THE **FUNNIER** IT IS!

CREATE YOUR OWN ALIENS, MONSTERS, FOOTBALLERS, T.V. STARS, ETC, ETC...

MORE CRAZY STUFF TO COME →

THE **NEXT** TIME YOU HAVE A PARTY, BARBECUE OR HOUSEWARMING—WHY NOT PRODUCE YOUR **OWN**, ORIGINAL INVITATIONS ?!

JUST DRAW YOUR DESIGN **ON CARD** AND SEND...

IF YOU WANT TO MAKE IT REALLY **SPECIAL** YOU COULD CUT IT OUT—OR **EVEN** MAKE A POP-UP VERSION!

FIREWORKS PARTY

FROM 6 — 9 AT STEVE'S BRING A FRIEND!

GOOD ADVICE ➔

HOW MANY TIMES HAVE I TOLD YOU—**NEVER** HOLD LIT FIREWORKS!!

OVER THE NEXT FEW PAGES I WILL INTRODUCE SOME SUPER CREATIVE **CARTOON WORKOUTS**, TO HELP YOUR CARTOON DRAWING **IMPROVE** IN LEAPS AND BOUNDS **!**

SEE WHAT **YOU** CAN DO WITH **• • •**

NUTTY NUMBERS?

ARTY ALPHABET

STRANGE SIGNS

THIS WAY TO THE JOKES

CREATIVE CLICHÉS?

ONCE YOU HAVE PRODUCED A FEW DOZEN
IDEAS USING LETTERS - **TRY** A FEW
NUTTY NUMBERS • • • •

IT'S **CRAZY** -
BUT IT'S **FUN**
AND IT WILL **HELP** YOUR CARTOONING !

WHEREVER WE GO WE ARE SURROUNDED BY
SIGNS — GIVING US INSTRUCTIONS, DIRECTIONS, INFORMATION...

★ ADD A FEW SIGNS TO **YOUR** CARTOONS.

TAKE AN ORDINARY **SIGN**, AND DO SOMETHING **CRAZY** WITH IT!

AAARRGHHH

'I SPEAK YOUR **WEIGHT**

YOUR DINNER IS IN THE **DOG**!

TRY SOME!

DANGER... QUICKSAND

★ KEEP OUT...
NO PARKING...
MIND THE GAP...
QUEUE HERE...

ETC... ETC... ETC....

CLICHÉS ARE CARTOON SITUATIONS THAT HAVE BEEN USED **MANY** TIMES BEFORE...

DESERT ISLAND
DOCTORS SURGERY
PRISON
THE STONE AGE
LEARNER DRIVERS
SUPERMARKET CHECKOUTS

THIS IS A **VERY** SHORT LIST AND I AM SURE YOU WILL BE ABLE TO ADD **LOTS** MORE!

ONE OF **MY** OWN FAVOURITE CLICHÉS IS THE **STONE AGE**...

(HERE IS ONE OF MY FAVOURITES)

HOW MANY TIMES HAVE I TOLD YOU — DON'T **BOLT** YOUR FOOD!

(I ALSO LIKE FRANKENSTEIN JOKES)

I **HATE** LEAP YEARS!

74

OVER THE NEXT FEW PAGES YOU WILL FIND A **HUGE** SELECTION OF "SPARE PARTS" THAT YOU CAN USE TO **HELP** BUILD YOUR VERY OWN CARTOON **UNIVERSE** • • •

LET'S START WITH SOME **FACES**

GO ON HAVE A GO!

NOW – SOME HANDS, FEET AND SHOES...

★ **TRY** SOME OF THESE AS A STARTING POINT.

HERE ARE SOME **MONSTER** PARTS FOR YOU TO **PLAY** AROUND WITH ...

...... AAAAARRRGGHH

I HAVE STARTED SOME COMIC STRIPS — NOW IT'S UP TO **YOU** TO FINISH THEM •••

REMEMBER TO USE LOTS OF EXPRESSIONS •••

THE LAST PART OF OUR "WIT SHARPENING" SECTION IS CALLED "**PUNCHLINES**"...

I HAVE COLLECTED SOME CARTOON CAPTIONS BELOW - ALL **YOU** HAVE TO DO IS DRAW A SUITABLE CARTOON FOR EACH **ONE** • • •

"NOT FISH AND CHIPS **AGAIN!**"

"WAITER - **TAKE** THIS AWAY."

"**THIS** IS YOUR HUSBAND?"

"PLENTY OF ROOM ON **TOP**"

"MIND THE **GAP** ~ AAARRGHH!"

"THIS IS A HOLD UP!"   "CATCH!"

"OF **COURSE** IT'S SAFE!"   "OOPS."

"YEAH? YOU AND WHO **ELSE**?!"

"ARE YOU **SURE** THIS IS FRESH?"

"READ THE INSTRUCTIONS AGAIN!"

"HOW MANY?!" "LISTEN....."

"I CAN'T SEE ANY VAMPIRES!"

... GOOD LUCK!

OH NO!

WE HAVE COME TO THE **END** OF CARTOONING IN COLOUR!

I HOPE THAT YOU HAVE **ENJOYED** THIS BOOK – AND I HOPE THAT IT HAS HELPED YOU TO GET STARTED IN **CARTOON** DRAWING!

BEST WISHES...

Peter Coupe

80